# BLIZZARD

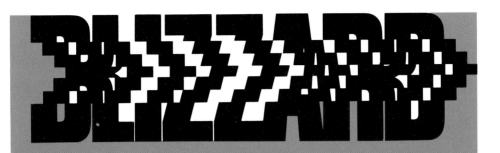

# BLIZZARD

**CHRISTOPHER LAMPTON**

THE MILLBROOK PRESS
BROOKFIELD, CT
A DISASTER! BOOK

Illustrations by Pat Scully

Photos courtesy of Superstock: pp. 6, 8–9, 16, 19, 36, 45, 48; National Weather Service: cover, pp. 11, 40 (top and bottom left); NOAA: pp. 12, 38; Library of Congress: p. 15; Photo Researchers: pp. 23 (Scott Camazine), 24–25 (Howard Bluestein), 28 (Van Bucher), 32 (Joseph Nettis), 40 (Hank Morgan), 50 (Art Twomey), 51 (Paolo Koch), 56 (Ted Clutter); Michael Ginsberg: p. 42; American Museum of Natural History: pp. 54, 55.

Cataloging-in-Publication Data

Lampton, Christopher
Blizzard / by Christopher Lampton

p.   cm.—(A Disaster! Book)
Bibliography p.    Includes index.
Summary: A blizzard occurs when severe snow is accompanied by low temperatures and wind. Details development, warning signs, destructive force and self protection for these winter disasters.
ISBN 1-56294-029-5     ISBN 0-395-63641-8 (pbk.)
1. Storms.  2. Meteorology.  3. Snow.  4. Weather.  I. Title.
II. Series.
551.5     1991

123456789 - WO - 96 95 94 93 92

# CONTENTS

# TOO MUCH
# SNOW

Sometimes, too much of a good thing can be a disaster. It's hard not to like snow. A snowstorm can be beautiful and fun to play in. It can lead to an unexpected vacation for schoolchildren. But too much snow can paralyze an entire country. It can cost businesses and governments millions of dollars, and even take lives. A little snow can be a lot of fun. But blizzards aren't much fun at all.

Do you live in Canada or the northern portion of the United States? Then you've probably seen more than a few snowstorms in your life. Maybe you've even been through a blizzard or two. And you probably came out of the experience just fine.

But think about the people who desperately needed to get to their jobs or to the hospital during the storm. What about the deliveries of food and other necessities that weren't made because the streets were blocked by snowdrifts? Think of the buildings that collapsed under the weight of tons of ice and snow.

Imagine the electric wires that fell to the ground when battered by winds and covered with ice. They can endanger passersby and cut off power to hundreds of people.

Snow is fun, but it's dangerous as well. And when severe snow is accompanied by extremely low temperatures and wind, we say that we are having a blizzard.

*Blizzards can make delivery of goods nearly impossible for trucks and create treacherous driving conditions for cars and buses.*

# A WINTER WONDERLAND

A snowstorm usually begins gently. Soft flakes float down from the sky accompanied by a gentle breeze. Usually, the weather is cold. It is not necessarily more than a few degrees below freezing, however. (Snowstorms are rare when the weather is extremely cold.) If you're like most young people, you probably stare out the window of your house and look at those first few flakes with excitement.

Quickly, however, a gentle snowfall can turn into almost a wall of snow. The falling flakes become so thick that you can no longer see the house across the street. The wind begins to drive the snow into great drifts. These block doorways and form impassable barriers across roads. Piles of snow can bury cars and trucks, making it nearly impossible to find transportation in an emergency.

The snow can continue to fall for many hours. It can recur repeatedly over a period of several days or even weeks. If the

*A gentle snowfall can soon turn
into almost a wall of snow.*

*Snowdrifts can block doorways and even windows.*

snow deposited by the previous storm hasn't melted in the meantime, the new snow simply piles on top of it. This makes the snowdrifts deeper still.

Deep snow is not the worst thing about a blizzard, however. There can be blizzards with relatively little snow. What actually makes a blizzard a blizzard? It is the combination of wind and cold that can cause snow to drift into great piles, dropping so-called windchill temperatures as low as 20° Fahrenheit (F) below zero.

# BLIZZARDS THEN AND NOW

Following are a few of the great blizzards that have struck the United States in years past.

One night in 1888, the city of New York was prepared for a mild winter storm. (Many blizzards begin with a weather forecast that calls for "light snow.") Almost 24 inches of snow fell out of the sky that night. The next morning, New Yorkers awoke to find their city completely paralyzed. The East River froze over. This allowed crowds of strollers to walk across the water between Manhattan and Brooklyn. But 400 people in New York and the surrounding area died from the freezing cold.

In 1940, a blizzard moved into the midwestern United States from Canada. It killed 100 people between the Rocky Mountains and Louisiana. Four months later, another blizzard killed 60 more people in the same area.

New York was struck again in 1947, when a late December storm covered the city with nearly 26 inches of snow. Traffic was

*The legendary blizzard of 1888. These New Yorkers are standing on top of a lamppost. The snowdrifts reach clear to the second story of the building.*

brought nearly to a standstill, and subways ran hours late. It was more than a week before the snow was removed, during which time 77 people died.

The winter of 1977–78 was a rough one for much of the United States. The eastern seaboard of the country, as well as the midwestern states, took a particularly awful beating that year. There were many blizzards, and icy conditions persisted for weeks at a time.

January of 1978 saw the entire state of Ohio buried under one of the worst snows the United States has ever seen. A national emergency was declared after 60 people died. A passenger train on its way to Florida ran into a snowdrift. It remained there for several days.

The 1978 storm that struck the city of Boston was a cause of celebration for many people. They happily sledded down the famous tourist spot Beacon Hill and put on cross-country skis to get through the center of town. But millions of dollars worth of property was destroyed by the storm, and 29 people died in the state of Massachusetts. More than 3,000 cars remained stuck in the snow for four days on a highway leading out of town.

New York City was once again buried under snow in 1978, this time 17.7 inches of the stuff. It was the sixth-worst storm in the city's history. The East Coast suffered significant damage from high winds and ice. Beachfront property was washed away. A historic ship in Boston Harbor even sank during one of the storms.

Opposite: *Property damage from a blizzard can be extensive, as shown in this photograph of a portion of the Maine coast after the blizzard of 1978.*

# WHY IT SNOWS

Snow is a lot like rain. Both are forms of what scientists call *precipitation.* Both are made out of water and both fall from the sky. And, in fact, it snows for pretty much the same reason that it rains. Snow and rain both happen when water is lifted into the sky to form clouds, then falls back to the ground. But how does water get lifted up into the sky in the first place?

Water is made up of tiny particles called *water molecules.* These particles are much too small to see with the naked eye. When water becomes warm, these tiny particles become excited. That is, they start moving around rapidly. A rapidly moving water molecule can jump right out of the water and into the air. It then becomes a molecule of *water vapor.* When this happens, we say that the water molecule has evaporated. The word *evaporated* literally means "turned into vapor."

Rain and snow happen when water is lifted up
into the sky to form clouds.

You've probably seen water evaporate without even realizing it. When the sun comes out after a rainstorm, for instance, the puddles of water on the ground and on the sidewalk dry up and disappear. Where does the water go when it disappears? It evaporates. That is, the water molecules escape into the air as water vapor. Because water vapor is invisible, you can't see the water molecules in the air. But they are there nonetheless.

The warmer the air is, the more molecules of water vapor it can hold. On a warm day, the air can gather up large quantities of water molecules as it passes over oceans and lakes and even mud puddles. We refer to the amount of water vapor in the air as the *humidity*.

As the air gathers more and more water vapor, we say that the humidity is rising. Sometimes, the air will gather up so much water vapor that it can't hold any more. Then we say that the humidity has reached 100 percent. This doesn't mean that the air has turned completely into water. It just means that it's holding all the water vapor that it is able to hold at its current temperature.

When air is warm, it tends to rise. Why? Because warm air is lighter than cold air. Warm air rises upward through the colder air around it like bubbles rising in boiling water. But a funny thing happens to the warm air as it rises. It gets colder. And the higher it gets, the colder it gets.

Cold air can't hold as much water vapor as warm air. When warm air full of water vapor rises upward and cools off, the water vapor leaves the air. It turns back into water. Usually, it turns into tiny droplets of water that are so small that they can float in the air without falling. When lots of these tiny droplets form in the same place, they create a *cloud*.

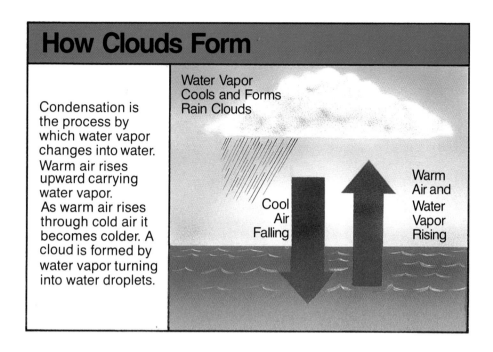

## How Clouds Form

Condensation is the process by which water vapor changes into water. Warm air rises upward carrying water vapor.
As warm air rises through cold air it becomes colder. A cloud is formed by water vapor turning into water droplets.

Water Vapor Cools and Forms Rain Clouds

Cool Air Falling

Warm Air and Water Vapor Rising

When water vapor turns back into liquid water, we say that it *condenses.* The process by which water vapor changes into water is called *condensation.*

# FALLING
# BACK TO
# EARTH

For rain or snow to occur, the water in the cloud has to fall back to the ground, or precipitate. This doesn't happen automatically. The tiny droplets are so small that the air holds them up quite nicely. In order for them to fall back to the ground, they must first form a droplet that is too large for the air to support.

It's very cold inside a cloud. Thus, the droplets that form quickly freeze up. Scientists who study the weather believe that the droplets usually freeze around tiny solid objects, often tiny crystals of ice. The tiny solid objects that the droplets form around are known as *freezing nuclei.* (The word *nuclei*—NOO-klee-eye—is the plural of the world *nucleus.* A nucleus is usually a hard core surrounded by some kind of shell.)

The result is a tiny piece of ice, floating in the cloud alongside the tiny droplets of water. When several pieces of ice inside a cloud bump together, they can form a *snowflake.* And when the

*Snowflakes preserved in plastic.*

snowflake is large and heavy enough, it falls back out of the cloud. Usually, it melts on the way to the ground and turns into rain. But if the weather is cold enough it will remain icy and will reach the ground as snow. Sometimes, the ice may get caught in an up-draft that will hold it inside the cloud for an unusually long time. Many layers of ice will form around the icy core. Eventually, these large chunks of ice will fall to the ground as *hail.*

Sometimes, the falling ice crystals will melt into water and then pass through another layer of cold air. Instead of refreezing, the water will become *supercooled*. This means the water is lowered to the freezing temperature without freezing. It will not ac-

*Freezing rain can create very hazardous conditions on the ground.*

tually freeze until it touches the ground. Then it will turn almost instantly to ice. This kind of precipitation is called *freezing rain* and can create very dangerous conditions on the ground for cars as well as for those traveling on foot.

# BLIZZARD CONDITIONS

For snow to take place, then, three things must happen. Water must be lifted high into the sky to form clouds. Snowflakes must form around freezing nuclei and fall back out of the cloud. And the air near the ground must be cold enough so that the flakes don't melt into rain.

The most important part of this process is the rising air that carries the water up into the sky. Air tends to rise mostly when the air pressure is low.

What is air pressure? It is the force with which air pushes down on the ground below it. We measure air pressure with a device called a *barometer,* which is a kind of scale for measuring the weight of the air. The heavier the air, the greater the air pressure. Warm air weighs less than cold air. So the air pressure tends to be greater when the air is colder.

More water rises into the air to form rain and snow when the air pressure is low. Thus, falling air pressure is a signal that a storm may be on the way. Rising air pressure, on the other hand, is a signal that the weather will be fair.

For a full-scale blizzard to take place, a *lot* of water must be lifted up into the air fairly quickly. The air near the ground must also be very cold. Cold air, you will remember, doesn't hold a lot of water. It also doesn't rise upward as readily as warm air. So a blizzard requires that cold air and warm air come together in a particular way. This usually happens at a cold front.

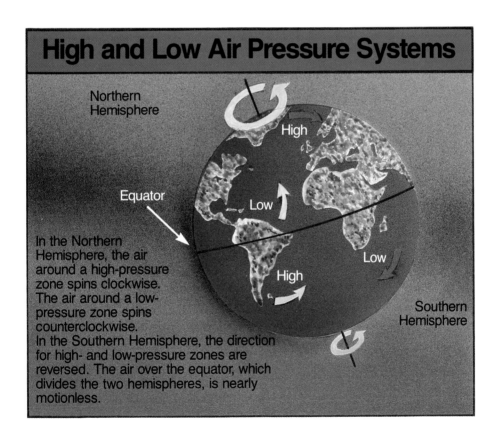

## High and Low Air Pressure Systems

Northern Hemisphere

High

Equator

Low

Low

High

Southern Hemisphere

In the Northern Hemisphere, the air around a high-pressure zone spins clockwise. The air around a low-pressure zone spins counterclockwise.
In the Southern Hemisphere, the direction for high- and low-pressure zones are reversed. The air over the equator, which divides the two hemispheres, is nearly motionless.

*A barometer is a device for measuring air pressure.*

What is a cold front? During World War I, scientists studying the weather in Europe noticed that air tended to move around in air masses. An *air mass* is a large section of air near the earth's surface. It is often hundreds or even thousands of miles wide. The temperature and air pressure are all pretty much the same throughout an air mass.

Air masses don't tend to mix together. When two air masses collide, they flatten out against one another. If one of the air masses is moving, it will often push the other mass ahead of it. The scientists who studied air masses during World War I were reminded of the way that two enemy armies came together at a battlefront. Thus, they referred to the place where two air masses came together as a front.

If a cold air mass is pushing a warm air mass, it's called a *cold front.* If a warm air mass is pushing a cold air mass, it's called a *warm front.*

The air pressure on one side of the front is usually different from the air pressure on the other side of the front. This causes the air in the higher pressure air mass to be "squeezed" into the lower pressure air mass. The result is a wind blowing across the front. A windy day is a sign that you are close to a front between two air masses.

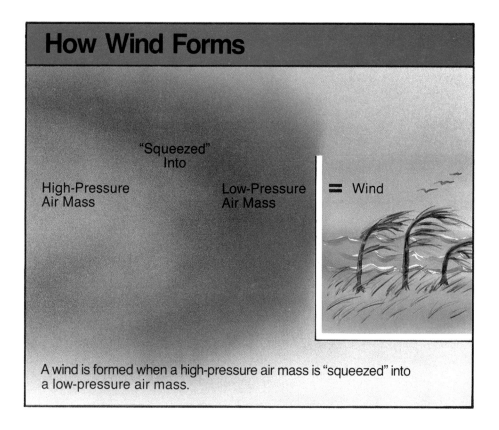

## How Wind Forms

"Squeezed" Into

High-Pressure Air Mass

Low-Pressure Air Mass

**=** Wind

A wind is formed when a high-pressure air mass is "squeezed" into a low-pressure air mass.

# How A Front Forms

Two air masses colliding flatten out against one another. Where they do, it is called a front. A cold air mass pushing a warm air mass is called a cold front. A warm air mass pushing a cold air mass is called a warm front.

Cold Air Mass →   Collide   ← Warm Air Mass   = A Front

When a cold air mass pushes a warm air mass ahead of it, the cold air mass tends to slip underneath the warm air mass. The warm air, in turn, rides up over the edge of the cold air. This forces the warm air to rise very quickly. The warm air carries water vapor up with it. Thick clouds will form in the rising warm air. When snowflakes form in these clouds, they fall back to the ground. But, because the warm air is riding over the top of the cold air, the flakes do not melt on their way back to the ground. Instead, they fall through the cold air and remain icy all the way back to earth.

In summer, when both air masses are too warm for snow, this can result in a thunderstorm. In winter, it results in a blizzard.

# BLIZZARDS
## AROUND
## THE WORLD

The cold air masses that produce blizzards usually come from the areas around the North and South poles. In the Northern Hemisphere, this means that blizzards are most common in the north. However, these cold air masses can often travel great distances to the south. The most common areas for blizzards are in the central United States, eastern and central Canada, and in the Soviet Union. But they can happen almost anyplace where temperatures fall below freezing.

Blizzards are actually not as common in the United States as in some other parts of the world. This is because even the points farthest north in the United States are not close enough to the arctic regions to experience cold air masses on a regular basis. Some experts believe that this makes blizzards in the United States more dangerous than, say, blizzards in Canada. Why? Because the United States is less prepared for them. People in

the United States are also less familiar with the hazards of blizzard conditions.

The U.S. National Weather Service defines a blizzard in terms of wind speed and temperature. To qualify as a blizzard, a snowstorm must have winds of at least 35 miles per hour (mph) and the temperature must be no higher than 20°F. To qualify as a severe blizzard, the winds must be at least 45 mph. The combination of 35-mph winds and 20° temperatures produces a windchill temperature of 20° below zero. Because strong winds are very common along a cold front, these conditions are not hard to come by in such a storm.

*Blizzards are most common*
*in the central and northeastern*
*United States.*

# BLIZZARD HAZARDS

Some of the dangers of a blizzard are obvious. Thick falling snow blocks roads and highways, causing transportation to grind almost to a halt. Airports can become snowbound. Railroad and subway tracks may be completely covered. Even a person traveling on foot in a snowstorm can become so lost that he or she will travel in circles for hours.

According to Ruth Kirk, author of the book *Snow,* Eskimos caught on foot in a snowstorm will stop traveling immediately, lest they become completely lost, even when relatively close to home. They will build a shelter out of snow and sit out the snowstorm for days, if necessary. To keep warm they will exercise briefly but not for so long that their clothes will become dangerously wet with perspiration. Once the storm is over, they will continue their journey.

The weight of the snow can be disastrous for buildings and other structures. Large quantities of snow can cause the roof of a building to collapse. Electric wires and telephone cables can snap under a load of heavy ice. Broadcast antennas can become choked with ice, threatening communications.

The falling temperatures are dangerous to human beings. They can easily develop *hypothermia* ("lowered body temperature") if caught in the storm without a source of heat. Motorists trapped on the road, for instance, will sometimes freeze to death in their cars. Or they might freeze while trying to walk from their cars to shelter. Ironically, some motorists may try to stay warm by running their automobile engines to provide heat. They may thus die of carbon monoxide poisoning from fumes that leak into the car from their car's exhaust system.

Some vehicles and special devices are designed for use in heavy snow. These can provide emergency transportation. Cross-country skis, obviously, are one means of moving around in snow. However, they require training before they can be used effectively. Snowshoes allow a person to walk on deep snow without sinking into it.

Perhaps the most effective form of transportation in a blizzard, however, is the *snowmobile.* This is a kind of powered sled with skilike runners. Snowmobiles are used primarily for sport, however, rather than emergency transportation.

Other dangers of a blizzard are not so obvious. The winds that are an important part of a blizzard can blow down electric poles and telephone lines or break windows. Blizzard winds have been known to reach hurricane force.

It's not unusual for a blizzard to bring a community to a complete standstill. Anyone who lives in the northern United States is accustomed to hearing cancellation reports on the radio during a snowstorm. School is typically suspended for the day, along with

The high winds that are part of
a blizzard can uproot trees.

most recreational activities. Offices are not always closed, but "liberal leave" policies are put in effect. That means that workers are excused from showing up for the day if they have difficulties traveling in the snow.

Blizzard conditions can linger long after the storm itself is over. Snow is heavy and difficult to remove from roads and buildings. If weather conditions take a turn for the better, the snow can melt and hazardous conditions can disappear almost magically. But if the weather remains cold, the problems associated with a blizzard can linger for many days, even weeks. Roads can remain blocked by ice and snow, power lines can remain unrepaired, frozen pipes can remain clogged. The result can adequately be termed a disaster.

THE
BANK
-11c
PORTLAND
SAVINGS

38

# ADVANCE WARNING

The Weather Bureau will do its best to let you know when a blizzard or other winter storm is coming. Here are a few of the warnings that you might hear on radio or TV when a major winter storm is expected:

A *blizzard warning* means that there will be snow driven by a wind of 35 mph or greater. Temperatures will remain at or below 20°F, probably over a fairly long period of time.

A *severe blizzard warning* means that the winds accompanying the snow will blow at 45 mph or greater. Temperatures will be 10°F or lower.

A *cold-wave warning* means that temperatures, with or without accompanying snow, will be falling to dangerous levels. This means different things depending on where you live. If you hear that a cold wave is on the way, however, be sure to take precautions. Don't go outside if it isn't necessary and bundle up warmly when you do.

A *livestock warning* tells farmers to bring cattle and other animals into sheltered areas, because a blizzard or a cold wave is on the way.

*The National Weather Service tracks winter storms using computers and satellites, and will issue warnings when a severe storm is on its way.*

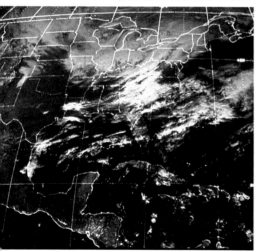

# WHAT TO DO IN CASE OF A BLIZZARD

First of all, stay inside! The weather outside may seem a lot less dangerous than it really is. If you have to go outside, take precautions against the cold. And watch out for *frostbite,* no matter what precautions you've taken against it.

The two main hazards of the cold are hypothermia and frostbite. To protect against hypothermia—a drastic lowering of the body's temperature—dress warmly so that the body's natural heat can't escape. Keep your limbs and your head dry. And stay awake. Hypothermia tends to make you drowsy. Carbohydrates are a good source of heat energy for the body, and they help you to stay awake. Munching on nuts and chocolate isn't a bad idea while traveling in the cold.

Frostbite can occur whenever your flesh is exposed to the cold air. Your skin can actually freeze and become permanently damaged. If the damage goes deep enough, you can even lose

The two main dangers of the cold, hypothermia and frostbite, can usually be
avoided by dressing in proper clothing.

part of your skin or an entire finger, toe, or limb. When your skin becomes numb, warm it up immediately. If you believe you've been frostbitten, seek medical help.

It's easy to become blinded by thick snow, making it impossible to tell where you are or where you are going. This condition is sometimes called a *whiteout,* because both the ground and the sky appear to be a featureless shade of white. In a really thick snowstorm, it's possible to get lost on a journey of less than a hundred feet—from one house to the next, for instance.

# WINDCHILL TEMPERATURE

We've mentioned windchill temperature several times in this book without defining it. You've probably heard the term used on weather reports. But what exactly *is* windchill temperature?

When the air around you is cold, your body temperature will tend to drop. This is one of the dangers of cold weather. If your body temperature drops too severely, you can be stricken with hypothermia.

The reason that your body temperature drops is that you lose body heat to the surrounding air. As long as the air is colder than your body, heat will tend to move outward from your body into the air around you. This will cause you to become colder.

Wind can speed up this process. We've all had the experience of standing in a breeze and feeling cooler. On a summer day, this can feel pleasant. On a cold winter day, it can be deadly.

*Cold winds can cause water to freeze
on plants and bushes.*

We lose body heat faster when the wind is blowing than when the wind is not blowing. Thus, the wind makes us feel colder. The windchill temperature is a measure of how cold we feel at a given temperature when the wind is blowing at a given speed. For instance, if the temperature is 25°F and the wind is blowing at 20 mph, then the windchill temperature is 3° below zero. Now that's cold!

# WINDCHILL EQUIVALENT TEMPERATURE TABLE

DRY BULB TEMPERATURE (°F)

| WIND VELOCITY (MPH) | 45 | 40 | 35 | 30 | 25 | 20 | 15 | 10 | 5 | 0 | -5 | -10 | -15 | -20 | -25 | -30 | -35 | -40 | -45 |
|---|---|---|---|---|---|---|---|---|---|---|---|---|---|---|---|---|---|---|---|
| 4 | 45 | 40 | 35 | 30 | 25 | 20 | 15 | 10 | 5 | 0 | -5 | -10 | -15 | -20 | -25 | -30 | -35 | -40 | -45 |
| 5 | 43 | 37 | 32 | 27 | 22 | 16 | 11 | 6 | 0 | -5 | -10 | -15 | -21 | -26 | -31 | -39 | -42 | -47 | -52 |
| 10 | 34 | 28 | 22 | 16 | 10 | 3 | -3 | -9 | -15 | -22 | -27 | -34 | -40 | -46 | -52 | -58 | -64 | -71 | -77 |
| 15 | 29 | 23 | 16 | 9 | 2 | -5 | -11 | -18 | -25 | -31 | -38 | -45 | -51 | -58 | -65 | -72 | -78 | -85 | -92 |
| 20 | 26 | 19 | 12 | 4 | -3 | -10 | -17 | -24 | -31 | -39 | -46 | -53 | -60 | -67 | -74 | -81 | -88 | -95 | -103 |
| 25 | 23 | 16 | 8 | 1 | -7 | -15 | -22 | -29 | -36 | -44 | -51 | -59 | -66 | -74 | -81 | -88 | -96 | -103 | -110 |
| 30 | 21 | 13 | 6 | -2 | -10 | -18 | -25 | -33 | -41 | -49 | -56 | -64 | -71 | -79 | -86 | -93 | -101 | -109 | -116 |
| 35 | 20 | 12 | 4 | -4 | -12 | -20 | -27 | -35 | -43 | -52 | -58 | -67 | -74 | -82 | -89 | -97 | -105 | -113 | -120 |
| 40 | 19 | 11 | 3 | -5 | -13 | -21 | -29 | -37 | -45 | -53 | -60 | -68 | -76 | -84 | -92 | -100 | -107 | -115 | -123 |
| 45 | 18 | 10 | 2 | -6 | -14 | -22 | -38 | -38 | -46 | -54 | -62 | -70 | -78 | -85 | -93 | -102 | -109 | -117 | -125 |

VERY COLD

BITTER COLD

EXTREME COLD

The chart on the facing page shows you what the windchill temperature is for various temperatures and wind speeds. Look up the temperature on the top of the chart, then check the wind speed on the left side of the chart. Follow the column leading down from the temperature and the row leading across from the wind speed. You'll find the windchill temperature at the point where they meet.

Keep the windchill temperature in mind next time you get ready to go out on a cold day. You might find that it's colder out than you think. You should bundle up accordingly. The windchill temperature is especially important during blizzards. Remember that a blizzard is a combination of snow, driving winds, and low temperatures. When these factors come together in the same storm, the windchill temperature can plunge to many degrees below zero!

# THE BEAUTY
# OF SNOW

Although blizzards can be disastrous, they have their bright side as well. There are few sights more beautiful than a snow-covered field. And few children are disappointed to hear that school has been cancelled for the day.

There are many forms of recreation associated with snow. In mountainous regions, fans of skiing react joyfully to word of the latest snowfall. They take their skis to the nearest ski resort and spend the day sliding down snow-covered slopes. Alas, skiing can be a fairly dangerous sport. Broken legs and arms are a well-known hazard.

A more deadly, but less appreciated, hazard of skiing is the *avalanche.* When snow lies several layers deep on a mountainside, a sudden vibration—the swish of passing skis or even the sound of loud laughter—can cause it to become suddenly dislodged. The falling snow can, in turn, dislodge more snow. The resulting cascade of icy particles can bury an unwary skier in

*German shepherds are quite suited to avalanche rescue work.*
Opposite: *An avalanche on Mount Everest in Nepal.*

mere seconds. Once trapped under the snow, a skier can only hope that a rescue party will find him or her before death by hypothermia occurs.

Dogs are commonly sent to sniff out skiers trapped beneath the snow. But many avalanche victims aren't found in time to save their lives. In 1954, for instance, an avalanche in Blons, Austria, buried 111 people, 64 of whom escaped (33 by digging themselves out of the snow). The remaining 47 could not be freed in time. Eight of those who were rescued later died of their injuries.

Sledding is a common neighborhood pastime after a snow-fall. A sled is simply a board mounted on skilike runners. If you live near a hill or graded road, you may have gone sledding after a snowstorm. But there are hazards associated with sledding, too. The runners on a sled can injure fingers and limbs. And a speeding sled can collide with an automobile venturing out into the icy streets.

*Sledding can be fun, but fingers can be injured on the runners that send the sled sliding down a slope.*

# SNOWFLAKES

Perhaps the most wonderful thing about snow are the snowflakes themselves. They have a beautiful symmetry that reminds us of images seen in a kaleidoscope. Most snowflakes are hexagonal—that is, they have six (usually identical) sides.

We have all been told that no two snowflakes are alike. This may be something of an exaggeration. (The standard answer to this assertion is, "Has anybody ever looked at all of them to be sure?") Certainly, there is an incredible variety of snowflake shapes. Most of them look quite striking when magnified.

In fact, there are people who have looked at more than a few different snowflakes. The American photographer Wilson Bentley began photographing snowflakes with the aid of a microscope in the 1880s. He continued doing this for many decades. In his lifetime, he took at least 6,000 such photos. More than 3,000 of them were included in the book *Snow Crystals,* published in 1931.

*Most snowflakes are hexagonal.*
*That is, they have six identical sides.*

A team of researchers at Hokkaido University in Japan photographed snow crystals throughout the 1930s and 1940s. They also developed methods for creating snow crystals artificially in the laboratory. By varying the temperature and humidity of the air, they were able to produce all the different types of snowflakes known.

*Snowflakes come in a dazzling variety
of shapes and sizes.*

In 1951, the Commission of Snow and Ice of the International Association of Hydrology (hydrology is the study of water) divided solid precipitation into ten different classes by shape. Seven of these apply to snow. They are plates, stellars (or stars), columns, needles, spatial dendrites, capped columns, and irregular crystals.

When the snowflakes reach the ground, they are often rearranged by the wind. The resulting drifts and dunes have a beauty all their own, much like wind-blown sand. As the snow melts and refreezes, icicles can form, glimmering like large diamonds as they hang from roofs and the bottoms of automobiles.

*As snow melts and refreezes,*
*icicles that look like large,*
*glittering diamonds can form.*

# GLOSSARY

*air mass*—a large section of air near the earth's surface in which the temperature and air pressure are fairly uniform.

*avalanche*—a sudden downfall of snow dislodged from the side of a mountain.

*barometer*—a device for measuring air pressure; literally, a scale for weighing air.

*cloud*—a collection of liquid water particles suspended in the air.

*cold front*—a front between two air masses in which the colder air mass is pushing the warmer air mass.

*condensation*—the changing of a gas, such as water vapor, into a liquid.

*evaporation*—the changing of a liquid, such as water, to a gas (or "vapor").

*freezing nuclei*—the tiny particles around which water freezes inside a cloud to form snowflakes and raindrops.

*freezing rain*—a rainstorm in which supercooled water freezes instantly upon contact with the ground.

*front*—the point at which two air masses come together but do not mix.

*frostbite*—damage to skin exposed to cold air.

*hail*—a large ice particle formed when frozen droplets of water are suspended inside a cloud for a long period of time by an updraft.

*humidity*—the percentage of water vapor in the air relative to the total amount of water vapor the air can hold.

*hypothermia*—a dangerous lowering of the body temperature in people exposed to severe cold weather conditions.

*nucleus*—a hard body at the center of some kind of shell, such as the nucleus of an atom, the nucleus of a living cell, or the freezing nucleus at the center of a frozen particle of water in a cloud.

*precipitation*—water, in frozen or liquid form, that falls out of the sky.

*snowflake*—the feathery mass of ice particles that falls out of a cloud during a snowstorm.

*supercooled*—a state of water; water that is lowered below the freezing temperature without actually freezing.

*warm front*—a front between two air masses in which the warmer air mass is pushing the colder air mass.

*water molecules*—the tiny particles of which water is made. Water molecules are in turn made up of hydrogen and oxygen atoms.

*water vapor*—the invisible gaseous form of water.

*whiteout*—a severe blizzard in which visibility becomes so limited that both the sky and the ground look to be an identical shade of white.

*windchill temperature*—a measure of how cold we feel at a given temperature when the wind is blowing at a given speed.

# RECOMMENDED READING

Lambert, David, and Ralph Hardy. *Weather and Its Work*. New York: Facts on File Publications, 1984.

Pettigrew, Mark. *Weather*. New York: Gloucester Press, 1987.

Webster, Vera. *Weather Experiments*. Chicago: Children's Press, 1982.

# INDEX